For A Rose
That Blooms In Fire

Isabel Rocio

Preface

THIS IS NOT a claim to wholeness. This is a progression from stagnant, to catharsis, to turned page. This is a reflection of a journey, one that is not meant to end at any point. This is for you, to know you aren't alone. More importantly, it is a push, for you to emerge from your comfort, and grow.

The journey I'm sharing with you is being told exactly how it happened for me—there was first a long period of darkness, and then a moment of realization, and the hopefulness and beauty that comes with healing and coming back to self. I invite you to skip ahead at any point to the second half of this book, starting on page 63, if you feel called to a space of comfort or empowerment. I understand that everyone's process is different, and though I hope you will at some point dive deeper within yourself and face any demons that need to be acknowledged, do so at *your* pace. Not all books need to be read front to back in chronological order; I always encourage breaking the rules.

I spent a lot of my life living in the mindset of a victim—I had decided that I was indefinitely a victim to my past, a victim to my depression, a victim to life's bad luck. It took me three years to realize I had a choice to overcome this mentality, another year after that to pull myself out of my own darkness and into a better life... and another year to finally feel like I'd shed an entirely different person from my soul. It's going to take me a lifetime to learn just a fraction of what I'm meant to learn about happiness and love and life; I trust that I'll never cease to grow.

Falling into an abusive relationship at fourteen, and remaining in that relationship for almost three years, feels like luck to me now; I learned very young what it means to lose myself to another person, and also how to fight to bring myself back—to be strong enough to realize I was never lost to begin with. I'm grateful I began learning how to persevere, and how to let go of relationships that only feel good on the surface, long before I ever learned how to do taxes or pay bills. Years later, and I'm still not entirely sure how to do my taxes, but I know damn well how to take care of myself—physically, mentally, and emotionally. I know how to thrive, even when I'm on my own...*especially* when I'm on my own.

This collection didn't begin with the intention of becoming a book; it began as a memory inside me, one that needed to be pulled out into the light, onto paper, where it begged for all the attention it required to be released. It began as therapy in the form of poetry, pain that danced its way into messy stanzas, and a lack of rhythm or any intention other than to be seen.

It had been years since I had actively thought about

the mental, emotional, and sexual abuse I had experienced during my relationship at such a young age. I believed that because it had been so long, and I wasn't in a severe state of depression any longer, that I had moved on. But each time I woke up from a dream or a match lit in my head while I was showering or driving or working, and I spilled scattered words onto paper or a note in my phone, I felt that there was more weight being lifted than I had realized was even there to begin with. I realized that the "good" feeling I had been cozied up in, was suppression, and complacency to a significantly traumatizing life experience—not *release.*

So, I continued to write. Eventually I realized I had so much to unpack, that I thought, "Shit, I could turn all this into a book!" And that fleeting idea kept coming up, kept needing to be acknowledged for what it really was, and for what it really could be.

For once, I trusted it. I trusted my intuition, and I went with it. The process of molding an abstract past into something tangible, even if no one might ever read it, felt right. It felt important to embrace and then let go of my past in this way; by taking pain and being able to understand it at a deep enough level to mold it into words—beautiful words, even. It was necessary to dive back into the darkness I'd ignored for so long, in order to dig it up and out of me, to make room for this new woman I was evolving into.

As the book started to unfold, I knew this needed to be shared, with anyone who needed to read it, anyone who could find comfort or hope in my words…I couldn't be alone, could I? The thought of not publishing the book began to scare me more than hiding it away from the world. Even if I could impact just one person by sharing my experience, that would have meant something to me. I want to see the world thrive, to share love and hope with people, especially women, who feel as though they have lost either of those for good. I want to start a conversation, about the form of abuse that no one talks about—the emotional abuse that a lot of us don't realize can exist, yet can destroy you more quietly than physical abuse; so many of us believe that the person who's abusing us, is the only person who could ever love us. While emotional abuse never makes headlines the way physical abuse does, it can be just as damaging, taking years or decades to heal from.

I want to bring to light the fact that sexual abuse doesn't just occur between strangers or within the walls of a first date; it can happen in long term, committed relationships, even amongst two people who have love for each other. And it does happen, all the time, behind the scenes of the taboo, uncomfortable conversations the media likes to trickle into the spotlight every now and then. I want to make sure every woman who has experienced sexual abuse, in any circumstance, understands that it is *not* her fault.

The biggest struggle I had along my journey was eradicating *shame* from my existence. Shame will eat a person alive if it isn't properly addressed; and it almost did for me. Shame is still being unraveled from my being, every day, from every encounter that threatens to wrap me back up within the past. Nowadays, shame is a face I recognize quick enough to release before it can consume me. I remind myself constantly of the absolute power I have, as a woman...as a human. When I glimpse that muddy, unrecognizable girl from the past,

I am reminded of how certain I was that I could never love myself as much as I do now; and how certain I am now that I can only love myself more.

This collection is a piece of my truth. The pain is not sugarcoated and the experiences are not romanticized. I hope that whatever comes up within you, as you journey through this book, is acknowledged, and tended to, the way it was as I wrote it. No experience is the same as another, and there is no right way to feel what I felt. My job as a poet is not to ask you to understand. My job is to allow you to feel both the reality of pain, as well as the liberation that comes from healing. And it will come. I promise.

I don't believe I know any more than the next person, about how to begin to love yourself again, or how to heal. This is not a claim to wholeness. This is a story about a rose that grew from ashes, with nothing but its own sunlight, and its own power to help it bloom. This is a rose, for you—to inspire you to grow, too.

Picking Roses

(To The Past, Lovers)

Sacrifices

Adults used to tell me
love means making sacrifices

None of them told me that
to love you and
keep you
would mean sacrificing
all of me

Filling Voids

There is so much loneliness
in your eyes.
how it consumes me

And fills you

Desire

Stealing away
in the night
losing sleep and
risking getting caught just to
taste your lips
how quickly I've become
addicted to you
how thrilling it is
to want you

To Be Needed

You're the first person to
look at me like
your life depended on it
as though the elixir for
your deepest pains
lies beneath the daydreams
in my eyes

Beginnings

I am a soft heart with
an ever-curious body
the confidence in your grip
when you pull me in
paints a question on my hips;
I wonder
how much my skin
has yet to learn

Healer's Curse

You'll be my lover
and I your sweet love
and I will love you how I was taught;
all-consuming, unconditionally
so trust me
trust me
when I swear
I will devote myself
to fixing you
even if it kills me

Taking Me

When I saw you
an utter need
for you
consumed me
I would do anything
be anything and
lose everything to have you

You read my mind
when we locked eyes and
took my notion quite
literally

Dressing Weeds
in Red Petals

Reciprocation

Is this love?
if I am the only one who
cares to understand
your mind?
if I am the only one who ever
dares to tend to
your heart?
if I am the only one trying to
fix you
when I am broken inside
too.

Subconscious Warnings

When I asked if you loved me
too
your hesitation only flickered in my mind;
I allowed your "yes" to consume me instead,
comfort and coax me back into
my daydreams
but that waver in your voice
tapped on the back of my head
where my intuition lay sleeping.
there is a part of me that is
alert now
fighting to push to the front of my mind
hoping I will see you
for what you really feel
who you really are

Certain Doubt

Our lips taste like uncertainty
I still cannot determine if this
doubt is seeping from your mouth
into mine
or from my mouth
into yours

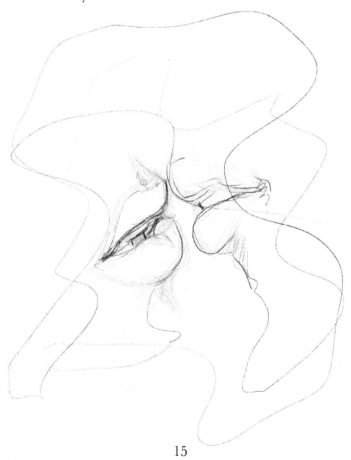

Trading Spaces

I fell into you
so blindly

And out of myself
so easily

I Didn't Know This Was a Lie

Be quick
you feel him drifting
fingers twitching for the door
snapping the pages closed and
eyeing the shelf again
your words were not enough
this time

Be quick
let him have a taste
a touch and
unwrap your covers for him
before he yawns into oblivion…
another lost lover.
intangible beauty is never enough.

I know it hurts but
tell your heart to quiet down
this is what he taught you
you are enough only if you
understand that love grows from
the gold in between your legs
not from the fluff within your mind

You Before Me

My mother hates you
my father wants to kill you
my brother has already
uncovered where you sleep

But they don't see you
they don't see your
sweet
if we just run away
no one can hurt you
and I'll pretend that
staying with you
isn't killing
me

Because it's you before me
you before
me
you
always before me

Immeasurable Distances

It's all been said before
your hand is just inches from mine
yet you feel so far away.
but I feel furthest from you
when you speak to me
when your eyes latch on to me
yet cannot bring themselves
to find my soul
and see

Intruder

If he left a kiss on my cheek
after breaking down the door,
does that kiss whisper,
"he didn't mean it"?

Or does it try desperately
to mouth its apology,
"he simply didn't care to
knock
before entering"

Making Love

The irony in your voice
when you call it making love
as if the words make the actions
seem less like
taking my body
and making of it
whatever you want

Daydreaming

A foolish young mind
I asked you to whisk me away
into love
handed you the key to my soul
gave up my integrity for
a fantasy

And you left me stranded
in the harshest reality
of falling in love with
not being loved

Every waking day turned into a dream and
all those dreams turned into
nightmares
and so I found more comfort
in remaining asleep

A Poisonous Healing

The moment I'd opened
my mouth
you'd stolen
my voice

Replaced my tongue with
your demands
knocked my teeth loose
each time I tried to
bite back

Filled my throat with
your over-flowing ego
until I felt I had no choice
but to swallow
to taste the poison
let it fill me to the brim
burn like whiskey in my stomach

How long was it
before I became accustomed
to the warmth?
how long was it
before I began to crave the way
you simmered in my blood

Not long
before my senses began to
deceive me
and I felt elated
drunk with the conviction
that I had discovered
the elixir of love

Gas-lighting

Somewhere between the lines
between fire and
you and I
I lost my mind.

You twisted me until
apologies began
gushing from my mouth
and I'd lost my grip
on why I had opened it
in the first place

Until eventually
it stopped opening
entirely
a fire put out
before it could begin

Four Winters

I've stopped keeping track
of the seasons
what is the point when
every moment I spend with you
I am cold

Unmasking

Today you looked at me
and all of the warmth you'd ever offered
flickered into the darkest contempt
I had ever seen any person's eyes hold

It is easier to believe
it was a trick of the light that
sent chills down my spine
rather than a very real mistake
of a predator forgetting to put his mask on
for his prey

Stumbling Through The Fog

Bewitched

When you ask me
am I happy
what do I need
I understand now
what you are really asking is
am I still bewitched enough
to make you happy
to give you
what you need

Freedom Cries

We sat in your car
listening to your favorite songs
and I listened as you
talked about
you
rain hammering against the windows
I watched the droplets
race gleefully down the glass
just as I did as a child
and I wondered
how sadness
could look so free

How desperately
I wanted to join the rain
so it could
show me

Narcissist

You were
exactly what you knew I
needed you to be
a shadow of smoke
donned in costume
chameleon and snake
trying on a new skin

You could smell insecurity on me
as pungent as raw meat
made yourself fit just right
in the scattered holes of my self-esteem

You had to fashion yourself a home
scratch your way out
and back in
enough times for my seams to tear
each tiny patch merging into one black hole
I believed you when you assured me
this damage was only temporary

You needed two bodies to
build your nest for one
carved it from
my conviction
padded it with my compassion
used my warmth as your shelter
only leaving me my bones

And I felt satisfied
to see you happy
in the comfort I had given you
in the comfort that destroyed me

The One Who Never Stays Gone

Every time I come close to
forgetting what it feels like to
lose you
you leave again
and i'm flooded with this pain
from wounds that
never really closed

But I keep waiting for you
to come back.
whether you stay or not
how deeply I believe that
the one who made the cuts
knows best how to
patch them up

Talking To Myself

What happens when you choke yourself
with your own emotions
for the sake of his composed breath
what happens when you silence your heart
just a moment too long
to keep his beating comfortably

Love does not thrive on suffering,
but a narcissist does.
if you must break your jaw
trying to coax love from his lips
look at your scars
you have to know in that clever mind,
there's no warmth in his heart for you
there's no warmth in him at all

Gratitude

Do you not see that I
am dying
to keep you alive?

Blue Roses

Every rose I have picked for you
is blue,
withered with the lackluster
gloom you've turned me in to

Disassociating

Don't say the word
that dirty word
even news headlines fail to form
it didn't happen
the way you picture it now
it never happened
at all
how could it have?
love was there as a witness,
right?
I won't believe that
love turned away
did she?
that she shoved herself behind the closet door
didn't let you see her face or
even feel her presence or
glimpse the tears on her cheeks
wouldn't allow you the chance
to determine whether her mangled mouth
stemmed from terror
or laughter
love didn't see it through
didn't see that single, halfhearted kiss
turn into one determined, ugly hand
clamped onto the back of your neck
didn't see your breath falter
into his dirty sheets
didn't witness your mind step quietly away
detach itself from your compromised body
didn't realize, until
your consciousness tapped her shoulder
your pride gasped into her ear

your armor meekly tucked itself
into her arms
love only witnessed the moment
when almost the entirety
of your being
had joined her in the closet
to cry

First Times

When you are young
every new experience feels like
flying
every moment is alight with
a newfound freedom
that fills every ounce of you

Was I so wrong to expect that
my first time
would feel just the same
I didn't expect that making love
would feel like
my mind fighting a battle
that my body couldn't muster

Sharing Sheets With the Lion

You fell asleep next to me
and for the first time in weeks
your breath rested
softly
in the nape of my neck
and I realized I could not
remain in the embrace of a man
who only allowed me peace
who only gave me a glimpse of
safety
when he was blissfully unaware
of my presence
how can I stay with a man
who I cannot rest alongside
out of fear for the moment
he awakes again

Ego's Nest

How familiar I have become
with ego
I allowed him into my home
made space for him to rest
fed his demands without question
allowed him to enter
the rooms in my mind which
I was meant to keep locked up
I made a home for him
protected him
until he grew too big for the both of us
and almost swallowed me whole
because I trusted his smile
when he introduced himself as
love

Did You Know

Keep the doors open
you're only kids
I was only fourteen
ask me once but, i'm too nervous
ask me twice but, i'm not ready
three times and
I'll say yes because
I love him
and he might not still
love me
if I don't

I was only fourteen
how did a mother not know
this young girl wasn't
safe in her son's arms
doesn't a mother protect
even if this child is not hers
but you turned a blind eye
as though you didn't really know
did you really not know?

Did you know your son was raised
to hear "no"
and plant "yes" into
a vulnerable, giving soul
too young to know her worth

Did you know your son was raised
to hear "no"
and carve "yes" into my hips
with the crushing weight of his hands
but he tells me it's okay
because he loves me

He loves me
there are scrapes around my waist
from his saying yes for me
because he loves me
there are tears in my body
where there should be a home
because he loves me

Did you know your son was raised
to think rape is love
and exclaim both in the same breath
he etched a lesson into my skin:
stay still
if you want him to stay

I've trained my nerves to stop feeling
my mind flinches and quiets itself
in this body whenever
a man is around and
sex tastes like pain now
because
he loved me

Did you know your son was raised
to break girls
in
to freeze their petals and
snap them in two
to swallow their softness whole
and fill the emptiness with a poison
that swims in their veins
for years

Cold Milk

Maybe I am the strongest person I know
for staying
but some days it takes me hours to
leave my bed
and maybe, then,
I am the best liar;
convinced of the stories I tell myself
to sleep better each night
so I can love you harder each day

Isolated

You keep leaving me
and I keep allowing you back in
and it seems that for every time you
come back
there is another friend
who must leave
another hand I once held
that I am no longer allowed to need
eventually, I fear
the next time you leave
the only person I will have
to run back to
is you

And that is precisely
what you want.

Setting Fire to the Meadow

Romanticizing Abuse

Abuse is not pretty
it is not a vague headline
that dances around an image too harsh for
the "real world"
despite the real world knowing
exactly what it looks like

It is not one text left on read
or a lack of attention paid for one day
it is not rough sex after arguing
and despite what hollywood likes to paint
it is not a brief scene that leaves you
uncomfortable but a little turned on

Abuse is not romantic.
it is surviving as a prisoner
in your own body
and trying to call it home
it is staying because you believe
this pain is the only
love you'll ever feel

It is suffocating on air
that used to be sweet
every time you inhale
because acid has tainted the air you need
scraping your throat as
a reminder that these lungs are no longer
yours

It is looking into a pair of eyes and hearing
"I love you"
while witnessing the remnants of their black rage
still clouding their gaze
it is hoping to relax into the same hands
that almost choked you the other day

Abuse is asking for a touch of
warmth
from a person that only knows
how to burn
but you've held onto the five days
of candlelight they gave you
when you first met them

It is believing you cannot run away
despite the chains on your ankles being
unlocked

Abuse is
expecting to be loved for
who you are
by a person that has stripped you
completely
of yourself

First Truths

The first truth
I ever learned about love
was that it's homicidal
knife to the throat
of naivety
gun to the head
of hope

The first truth
I ever learned about Love
was that it's selfish
a whirlpool
spiraling directly underneath
my identity

You beat my heart into submission
so that every time, I
would lick my wounds
and kiss you again

After I left you
the scars still lingered.
I ignored their sting.
the warnings they heeded
each time I tried to
love again

How many more scars will I bare
before
I am certain of
whether I am plagued with
naïvety
or if maybe, there are sweeter
truths
to be taught

Deja Vu

After I left you
I didn't feel free
no weight lifted off my shoulders
elation glided right over my head
instead of kissing it

Because
you were still with me
in every person I tried to love
you sank your teeth into each
moment that should have been
soft and fluid and new
poisoned it with
bitter, haunting
pause

You instilled hesitation in me
painted my love in charcoal fear so
every time I touched a hand
that wasn't yours
I left behind a stain
that served to remind me
I needed to unravel you
from my being
before I could love
anyone else

Magician

There was nothing
profound about you
except for your exceptional ability
to trick my eyes into
seeing magic in you

And you knew I foolishly
believed
loving you would
make me magic too

Addictions

I didn't love you
but a mind can fool a person
into feeling anything
when they're intoxicated

The problem was
I didn't know when to stop
drinking you
no matter how foul your love
tasted on my tongue
the next morning

It becomes harder to stop
feeling a thing that never really
felt good
when you're so full of the burn
that you start to forget
what your own
purity tastes like

Blind Faith

Our love was spiritual
until you reminded me of
why I never believed in a god---
blind faith can kill a person

The Abuser

The gentlest lover found me
broken
held me in the midst of
your aftermath
it was only when I
lashed out at him
stifled his needs for my own
that I realized
it was not your war I was battling
it was my own
I was fighting to remain
me
fighting desperately against
becoming
you

And the Abused

I saw your reflection
in my lover's eyes
the other night when I
screamed at him
for the pain
you had caused me
and for a moment
I understood what it meant
to hurt someone
because it is easier than
coming to terms with
your own pain

Self-Love in Love

I used to tell you
"I don't know who I would be without you"
a profession of my love for you
a confession of a lack of love for myself

But handing someone the tool to
define me
means also handing them the weapon
to destroy me

Ocean Trenches

My love for you was true
spun from the threads of my soul
as real as the skin on my back
you had never hurt me the way he had
you were the gentlest lover
nurturing and comforting and
present.
you loved me as authentically as I you
our chemistry felt spiritual
in my godless heart

Where did you go?
I must have lost your attention
in the midst of your despair
or in the clouds of my own
I hadn't yet fixed the parts of me
he had shattered
and you hadn't realized
you were broken until I
showed you what
broken looked like

Love lost itself in a shipwreck
of two rocky souls unable to
love the oceans in themselves
self-awareness killed us
or maybe a lack thereof
before we could finish growing
together
at least I have faith that our death
helped me grow
helped you grow
even if we will never know
how expansive our world
could have been
had we grown as
one

Promise Ring

You should have said
"I will try"
when you spoke of caring for me
as tenderly and for as long
as you lived

It was the word "promise"
that smashed me into pieces
hope
is a lot less fragile
than belief;

So, I suppose your lack of belief
in the promise you made me
is precisely why you broke it
so easily

Wallowing

Some days I find myself
tearing open the pin-sized hole
you left in me
until it is big enough for me to crawl into
cross my legs and feel the weight
of my emptiness

These days I find comfort
in removing myself
from myself
placing the responsibility of my
stained-glass soul in your hands
it is easier to blame broken glass on
your carelessness
and not on my inability to
protect myself

Yes some days I miss you
I feel the lack of your presence as painfully
as though you'd stolen a lung
carved it out of my softness and
took it with you as a token

Yes some days I miss you
stooping low enough
to wonder
why I should miss a person
who makes me miss
myself

Reflections

Why couldn't you see the
beauty in me?

Or is it I who doesn't
see it in myself?

Too Soft

Half of me wants to see you bleed out
the way I did for you
until you are completely empty
of me
of love
half of me knows I would bandage
your wound
before you ever felt its sting
my heart remains too soft
too forgiving
for a man who dropped our future
into the depths of his own uncertainty

Remnants

Standing in this room of broken things
there are handwritten letters and empty coffee cups
unmade beds and a record player
stuck on our favorite song
all things that signify an ending
the closing of smaller doors that were meant to
open again
on another day
but never did
I've lost track of the moments
that ended at a point where they should have began
of the love I wanted to give but never did
of the things that were better left unsaid
but would've broken through the silence
that we left
standing in this room of broken things
all I see is you
and me

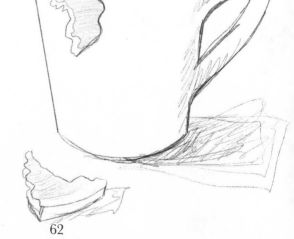

Two Faces

His hands were all over me but
he never felt me
eyes glazed over, distant
apathy playing as intimacy;
a young fool,
I let him treat my body
as a means to an end.

So when you came along
gently asking me to sit there
exposed and vulnerable
and allow you to soak in every inch of me
with your eyes
before I dare let you appreciate me
with your hands
I mistook it for love

Hindsight speaks the truth that
neither of you
ever really saw me, past my flesh.
you were just better
at feigning admiration.
my mind is recognizing
how to protect the skin
it lives in
from both kinds of men
both kinds of manipulation.

Inhaling A Silhouette

Some say you can taste smells
I didn't quite understand until
I inhaled the salt of your skin
a jolt in the calm of the night
the sweetness of your breath was mine
alone
no one told me,
you can taste memories too

Anger is Self-Inflicted

I was suffocating until I realized
it was my own hands,
not yours,
that were wrapped around my neck

The tighter the grip
the more comfort I felt
white knuckles and
scorching palms
reminded me of the way
you used to hold me

Can you imagine how long it took me
to finally loosen my grip
and finally let go of
anger
to finally choose control
over blame

Endings

It was not I who wished
to die
it was my soul
which desperately wished
to be reborn
to break out of the thick blanket of
suffering it had sewn itself
and to delicately transform into a new skin
a skin made from the silk of revelation
stitched with the threads of old wounds
wounds that will always be carried
but must never add weight to existence
a skin set in place with the fire
of liberation

It was a shadow
of a reflection of me
which dared to die
and so it did

Sewing Seeds in Ashes

(To A Reflection of Me)

New Perspectives

Losing you meant
meeting myself
again

Me Before You

The problem was never about deciding
whether I loved you enough to stay
it was about deciding whether
I loved myself enough to
leave

Hazy Recollections

How strange
it feels
to know that yesterday, I was
your tomorrow

And today I can barely
fathom
the hue of your
eyes

The Wrong Rose

I wonder
if you fantasize of
my nectar
when you're sipping on
hers

How bittersweet it must be
to miss me

To My Past Self

You may look back and wish
you'd never kissed him
because that kiss and
every one after that continuously
emptied you of
yourself

But I promise this pain will bring peace
I would not wish the same
pain upon you ever again
but if you had not endured it
there would be no scars on you
marking where flowers should be
planted

I cannot wait
until you look at yourself
and witness how miraculous
your petals appear
after sprouting from the depths
of hopelessness

Eviction

Shame made a home in me
burrowed itself deep in my foundation
it tried to melt the floors
failed to force the walls down
it screamed
and fought
to set itself on fire
in an attempt to disintegrate my being.

Eventually it gave up on destruction;
it chipped away at my coating of paint,
left a hole in the wall
pulled a few strings from the rug,
cracked a window and tilted the floor
just a little bit at an angle.
enough to drive me mad for a moment
furiously watching my mind roll from one side of
the room
to the other

I kept stumbling into empty rooms
that weren't there before
flicking lights on and off
and on
and off
wanting to navigate my vessel
but not wanting to witness the damage
I lived claustrophobic in my own head
disgusted with my failed attempts
to clean up the mess
I had let shame make in me

I almost moved out
because the wind kept whispering through the
ceiling,
shame delivering its eviction notice

then I realized
the only thing really wrong
was too much dust coating the windows,
keeping the light out,
gathering like a blanket on my soul

So I grabbed the broom
and swept it out
and planted flowers
in the wall

Burn

You bound shame around me
a thick cloak of fire
hoping I would suffocate
and submit

But within the darkness, I forged
freedom.
you cannot set fire to a woman
who was made to burn

Being Both Seed And Sunlight

When There Is Intuition

A woman in control
of herself
knows when to release control
of a lover
who is not meant to stay

Seasons

You loved me in the midst of
a venomous summer
but my love for me began in
spring
and will flourish past
another man's winter

The seasons can't
hurt me anymore
when I am the force
that controls them

Phantom

Ever since you left
I've become wild,
in love with myself
finding ecstasy in
dancing with nothing but my soul as a partner

Every now and then
in between songs
I feel your hands on my waist,
your phantom presence

And before I can think to miss you
I wonder if I've grown so strong that
you can feel my body's rhythm
pulsing from miles away

And I wonder how deeply
you ache

When Gazing in the Wrong Person's Eyes

You will never see yourself for
who you are
through an image of
what they want you to be

The Reason I Forgive You

Your biggest shadow
is your ego.
it clings to you
like a leech,
consumes you,
turns blood into concrete
in your veins.
covers your eyes with
the notion that it is
everyone else
but you
who can't see

Anger is a weapon for the Ego
and it is the only one that will
damage you deeper
than the person you meant to wound

Embracing Me

The moment I decided to
choose me
over you
birds miraculously grew from concrete
and flowers flew down from the clouds

Erasing You

Creating art was not
meant to be painful
but I have re-lived every stroke of your
torment
through every word I have dotted
on to these pages
until the lines and the
metaphors
made you a bit less
real in my head

And you will never look eloquent on paper
but your memory is
safer there
you can do no harm when I have
tossed you into the oblivion---
another sad tale of a man
who tried to break a woman

Reconditioning

My mind is still learning to trust that
not every man's hands are vultures that
prey without permission
and my body is still understanding
that the best hands to
soften and reframe this belief
do not belong to even the most
tender man alive
they belong
to me

Redefining Truth

The first truths
I ever learned about love
have sputtered and perished
an angry flame set free
by the river in me
that found love wading
patiently among the rocks

Among all your chaos
I understood that love
is a force
that can either soothe
or destroy
if I allow it the power to

And living a life in
fear of love
is just the same as
living a life in
fear of
myself

In Good Company

Your absence
has somehow made me feel
less alone

Holding Ghosts

There are ghosts in my chest
that refuse to be ignored
so alive they make me pinch my own skin
to make sure I am still real
there are ghosts in my chest
that toss and turn
rattling my insides just for some
attention

I should not have ghosts in my chest
that hold tight to my heart
and call that moving on
I should not have memories locked up inside
so vivid they blur what's in front of me
and call that letting go
I should not have shadows hidden under covers
and call that enlightenment

So, I took the ghosts
and the memories
and sat with them
I spoke with the shadows in me
and held them.
the ghosts in my chest
felt the relief of open air in my
nurturing hands.
felt the warmth of budding roses in my
listening ears.
and then, without a fight,
they left, peacefully.

The ghosts in my chest only let me
breathe
when I had allowed them
to breathe
with me.

I Will Not Mourn

You will not be
the last time
I fell in love
a new name will lay itself
upon my tongue
lounging sweetly,
vividly
atop a faint
memory of you

And maybe a part of your soul
will always come lay to rest
behind my closed eyes
in the dark of every night
but when morning kisses me
and that part of you
is gone
I promise I will not mourn its
absence

Rejoice In Being

The moment I stopped crying
over who I wished I was
and started embracing
who I am
was the moment my magic escaped
where it hid among my mind's shadows
and burst into the sky, a million stars aflame,
dancing above my head

That night they spoke to me
whispering sweetly through night's vacancy
I am love
I am strength
I am infinite.

And so I listened.
and so I was.

For The Record

It's been a while
the note of your voice is no longer
a lullaby in my ears
nor does it bring me sorrow
and his, hasn't even made a sound
I am too full with my own sweet music
to mourn over the loss of any lovers'

You haven't called
and I've stopped dreaming you would
I know you still check in on me
and I've stopped parading
behind your screen, delicately
molding a façade for you to see
the only person I need to
prove myself to
is myself

My smile feels like heaven
and my warmth is unwavering
and I've stopped needing someone
to feel it for me
just to know it's there

But just for the record
I am living
beautifully, slowly
fully
in my own arms
when a year ago I
swore I could not bloom
without your sunlight

And just for the record
I've changed
I taste like freedom,
this sugar in my skin
is the kind of sweet
that keeps you awake at night
vanilla and honey daydreams
I am the kind of sweet
you'll never get to know
because you coated your tongue
in salt
the moment you lost me

Picking Shadows

Searching for petals among ashes
might seem an easy, silly task
but the irony of searching for
remnants of life among death
entices madness.

It is only after the severe pain
of the past,
has coated your hands and feet,
and crawled into your lungs,
that you will realize,

We must die countless times
in order to discover our
true soul,
pulsing resiliently
among the old

Learning In Love

I can't possibly regret
loving you.
there is no such thing
as wasted time
and if there were such a thing
as wasted love
I would only be half
of who I've become
from learning to love me
through loving the
wrong one

Embodying Fire

There is a phoenix
caressing her spine
allowing her to rise up
from her own demise,
from the wreck you tried
to bury her with.

You have not seen power
until you have witnessed
a soft thing
unleash a fire
from her eyes

The Keeper

The act of
entering into someone's heart
should never lock you outside of your own

I will never again lose the key to my mind
as easily as I had slipped it under
my blind devotion to you

I will never again crouch before a single flame
thinking it will keep me warmer
than the sky ablaze with a thousand suns
inside my own heart

After Dark

There are some mornings when day breaks
like water in my hands
a proud sunrise shatters the night
reminding me just how far I have come
from a love that once leaked darkness into every
new day

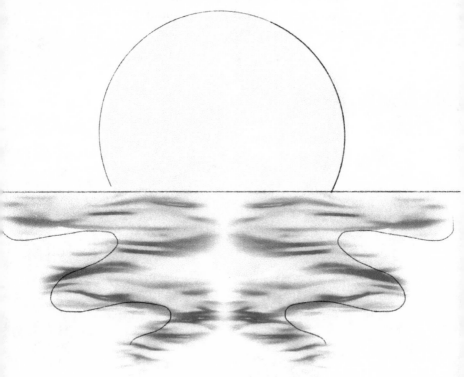

Watering The Nurturer

I can't expect someone
to love me despite my faults
if I myself do not see those faults
as precious seeds waiting
to be nurtured

I cannot ask for someone to
grow with me
if I haven't first made the choice
to grow on my own

Power

In the reality of my own mind,
no blame on you will suffice
to soothe the aches or the cries
hammering the inside of my soul
you don't live in my mind,
I do.
I do.
and that is the one truth you cannot
could not
take away,
the truth that I am
painfully and
peacefully
dreadfully and
lovingly
alone in my own mind;
the only one
who can heal me from the inside.
the only one with the key.

Blooming From Within

A Message For You

Please understand,
you are not his abuse
you are not his cruelty
you are not a product of
the treatment you were too
familiar with to get away from
for so long

You are not an extension
of his unhealed trauma
and you are not defined
by your own
learning from your pain
does not have to mean
relying on it to exist

Nature's Power

Watch,
as I slip out of your fingers
and into something
fresh

Specks of sunlight crackle softly
atop my skin
each diamond kiss hoping to
make a home out of me

You could learn something
from the way daylight graces me
only touching me when I've
leaned into its warmth

You could learn something
from the way the blossoms gaze up at me
knowing full well
where their beauty stems from

Understand,
the only way to truly
feel a woman
is to grasp the divinity she stems from

Musings

I pictured myself
as every fantastic woman
in the movies
with eyes like fire and a mind
like the inside of the sky
I pictured myself
as a woman to yearn for
without needing the man there to
yearn for me
I pictured myself as
a woman to dream of during
every waking moment
I became both the dreamer
and the muse, dancing among
sleep-ridden clouds
I focused so intensely
on becoming the woman
of my dreams
and when I opened my eyes,
I caught a glimpse of myself in the mirror
and knew exactly what it meant
to fall in love
with the woman I saw

A Lover's Job is Not to Heal

The most attentive hands and
kindest words
can create a warm
façade around you
but they can never
break through skin
to fill your heart

The greatest love your body can know
lies within it
not outside of it

Looking Up At Me

I saw fear flicker in his eyes
when I said "no" without a pause in my breath
and I realized that
a man in fear of my power
falls hand in hand with his
desire to destroy it

The one for me will
lean into my heat, and rest
instead of pouring the waters of
aggression upon it
in an attempt to
put it out

Colors

You coated me in black and grey
dubbed me an enigma unworthy of being
discovered

I have since been meditating on myself
and found within my depths
that my spirit is the fiercest red in its conviction
and my compassion boasts a brighter yellow than
the sun you tried to steal from me

The little taste of peace I found in leaving you
swims in the most supple ocean blue and
I'd never seen a sweeter hue until I glimpsed
the magic my mind was made of

You kept me from witnessing how
effortlessly my love mimics all the
palest pinks and brightest oranges of a sunset
closed my eyes to the brilliant flecks of lilac that
were
hidden timidly within my aura

If an angel painted herself in every color
the human eye can see
she would still only be nearly
as otherworldly
as me

To My Next Lover

I don't need you to fix me
just kiss me where my seams start to loosen;
remind me to continue
fixing myself

Anointed

It took candlelit nights
by myself
to reconnect to my body's
wisdom
after so long of feeling it was
less than divine

There is not a thing anyone
can teach me about this temple
that I am not capable
of teaching myself
how sacred my skin feels
when I am touching
my soul

Intuition

If your body
shrinks in his presence
listen to its defiance.
what makes you think
he will not poison you
from the inside out

Softer Standards

My next lover
must have daisies in his chest
kissing every one of his ribs
blooming in all the spots the world wants to
smother
so perhaps my softness will neither
break him nor scare him
it will be a
home to him
and perhaps we may grow
together

The Impossible

I knew I held strength
when in the darkest,
coldest corner of my mind
I managed to make flowers
grow

I witnessed the sun open
at the rise of a blossom

To Know Love

I hoped love would find me
yet did not think I deserved
its presence

I've learned that
love must live in us
lay its head down on our pain
curl itself up in our fears
be fed so it can feed us
cross its ankles and
feel us

Before it can ever
know us

If we are strangers to love
how will we ever
take its hand
without hesitation
when it reaches from
the soul of a stranger?

Harvesting Divinity

New Life

There is a new life
waiting around the corner
from where you huddle safely amongst your pain

It is time you decide which you fear most:
pursuing the unknown ahead of you
or never even touching
the life
that belongs to you

A Rebellion At Dawn

This subtle act of rebellion
I am free to love myself as fiercely
and with as much resilience
as the vibrantly green sprout that blooms from
a crack in two rocks
against the beating of an angry river
this subtle act of rebellion
I am free to kiss my wounds into
effervescent petals
against the will of
winter's unkindest frost

You told me I would never find
a love like yours
yet I have found pure,
unconditional love
within myself
against the burn of every wound
you bared in me
you knew I was as willful
as nature
you just never believed
I would one day know it too

Volumes

If my conviction is too loud for you
allow me to speak a bit louder
for I have spent too long
silencing myself
to be bothered by those who are terrified
of the volume a woman can reach
when she loves herself

A Brighter Star

You are made from the dust of stars
magic being birthed from every step you take
the sky you're so enamored by is alight with
death and rebirth,
the cosmos rearranging her skin every chance she
gets
but each night when you gaze up,
towards divinity,
you fail to recognize yourself as a reflection of what
you see
you fail to recognize that your brilliance comes
from falling and flickering,
as stars do
your brilliance sits at the center of a room
filled with every moment a part of you has burnt
out,
just so a brighter star could illuminate your infinite
soul
and there may have been times when
five stars died out at once,
and the darkness threatened to consume you,
but that only made the birth of
ten more
that much more breathtaking.
how remarkable it is; your ability to
bring yourself back to life,
more powerful than before

Where Intimacy Begins

When a lover lies before you
you desire to study every inch of them
to know their skin and their troubles
as deeply as your own
but when was the last time you
asked the same intimacy of yourself
exposed you to you and understood.
woman,
there is a relationship so deeply engrained
in your own skin,
no lover's eyes could ever trace where in your body
it began
no lover's hands could feel just how
deep you go
there are a thousand truths embedded
in your flesh, if you would only
seek them out
the answers to the pain your body cries of
lie only a moment beneath where your scars start
to peek through
if you would just linger a while longer and
listen
to the music that sings beneath
every dirty fingerprint that has tainted your
softness
hear the roots in your chest
expanding and reaching through the soil
in your bones
trying to tell you
trying to tell itself
of how much love you house
if you would only understand that the body
you claim has been bent and broken
under the weight of all the wrong lovers
is the same body that is fighting to prove to you

it was never broken
you
were never broken
you were wilting but not fallen
from pouring too much water
on weeds that
all the wrong lovers had planted in your mind

Letting What Is, Be

I cannot explain how
I came to love myself

A person can sit on a mountaintop
and ask
how and why the sun chooses to rise

But the colors become godlier
when one stops questioning a thing of
beauty and simply
allows it to
be

A Life Not Quite Finished

The smell of smoke
dances in the air
my eyes milky with tears
at the sight of embers
drifting freely up to join the stars

There's been a death
and I am celebrating it.
I am celebrating the death of
the girl who refused to love herself
of the girl who simply didn't know how

I am celebrating the life
of the girl who nearly
let pain be the fire that consumed her
and instead gave herself up to
the hands of rebirth

I am celebrating the ashes
of a past that stayed behind
to make room for a new flame
a flame lit by the woman
who moves with the intention to live,
not survive

The woman who is unashamed
of her dark, because she's seen it coax out
the light
the woman who is not afraid
to die;

The woman who
dares to be
reborn

CPSIA information can be obtained
at www.ICGtesting.com
Printed in the USA
LVHW090023061220
673447LV00012B/475